FAREWELL TO FEAR
The Memoirs of a Holocaust Survivor
with photo illustrations

by Ena Tarrasch and Thel Spencer

Sherrie,

My mom wrote her memoirs for her grandchildren & I wanted to share some of her story with you. This is just a fragment of the wonderful things she accomplished and overcame during her lifetime. She would be thrilled to know that you provided the opportunity for Trevor & Joel to experience the March of the Living.

Thank you.

Mimi Tarrasch

ACKNOWLEDGMENTS

Our thanks to Editor Rebecca Black, formerly a pupil in Ena Tarrasch's preschool, to Jim Young, Jr. for manuscript layout, and to Janet Abbey for cover design. Their help was above and beyond invaluable.

Library of Congress Cataloging-in-Publication Data

Tarrasch, Ena, 1913-
    Farewell to Fear : the memoirs of a Holo-
caust survivor / by Ena Tarrasch and Thel Spencer; with foreword by Rabbi Rita Sherwin.
    128 p. cm.
    Includes index.
ISBN 0-87714-190-8
    1. Tarrasch, Ena, 1913-   . 2. Jews--Mis-
souri--Springfield--Biography. 3. Refugees,
Jewish--Missouri--Springfield--Biography.
4. Jews--Germany--Biography. 5. Germany--
Biography. 6. Springfield (Mo.)--Biography.
I. Spencer, Thel. II. Title.
F474.S7T37 1997
977.8'78--DC21   97-341
                                      CIP

Table of Contents

FOREWORD

The first time I met Ena Tarrasch, we spoke about her volunteer work at the federal prison here. Ena told me that she visited the inmates because she is a Holocaust survivor. She explained that reaching out to unfortunate people was her attempt to come to grips with the haunting question of why, while millions of other people perished, she survived.

During the years that Ena and I have gotten to know each other, the conversation has continued to intrigue me. What experiences, I wondered, had Ena undergone? Against what terrors had she struggled? And, most important, how had she managed to emerge triumphant, filled not with bitterness and hate, but with compassion and love?

Therefore, it was with great curiosity that I began to read Ena's memoirs, which turned out to be even more fascinating than I had anticipated. Sharing memories, recounting adventures and making history come alive, Ena maintains a keen eye and a dry wit. Her courage--- the courage to overcome fear, the courage to embrace happiness---is an inspiration to us all.

In her diary, Anne Frank wrote: "Give of yourself...you can always give something, even if it is only kindness...No one has ever become poor from giving." Ena Tarrasch's memoirs are proof that, indeed, in giving, one becomes rich.

Thank you, Ena, for giving us <u>Farewell to Fear.</u>

Rabbi Rita Sherwin, Temple Israel, Springfield, Missouri
November 10, 1996 - Heshvan 28, 5757

INTRODUCTION

Fear is a devastating thing. It is constant, following you through the day and disturbing your sleep at night. Fear can attack any part of your body, even paralyze you while it eats away at your life like a cancer. There are imaginary fears and real fears and I have been terrorized by both...and only by becoming a strong, independent woman with a will to survive could I stand against those fears and come to grips with the unanswered question of why I was spared and why so many other Jews perished in the Holocaust. Finally, many years later, marriage, close friendships and the achievement of lifelong goals have brought my life back full circle to love and contentment.

"...there are imaginary fears and real fears
and I have been terrorized by both..."

ONE
The Beginning

The crucible that was the Holocaust seared deep into the life of every Jew, scarring us forever and I am no exception. It tore away the life my parents had imagined and prepared for me in a single moment, leaving desperation and despair tempered only by fear for a very long time. But before the desperation and despair, there was the delicate crystal cradle of my early life.

An only child born to parents over forty, I was a cherished little princess. My father, Henry Kaff, was an Austrian citizen who had lived in Belgium for twenty-three years with my mother, Meta Hedwig Kaff, who became an Austrian citizen when she married my father. Father had stubbornly refused to give up his Austrian citizenship because he so loved the Kaiser, and when I was born in Brussels on October 23, 1913, I became one also. My parents had waited for a child for eighteen years and my father was enchanted with his beautiful little daughter. Bursting with pride he went to the courthouse to register my birth certificate, giving my name as "Bettina." Not being familiar with it, the Belgian clerk asked my father to choose another name. He flew into a rage and told them to "name her

'Elizabeth' or anything else you choose...for me she is always Bettina!" My father never spoke of this to me and I was Ena to my parents all their lives. I never knew the name on my birth certificate until I was twenty-one years old.

My father was a successful business man and so we had money and social position. My mother had been educated in a private Swiss finishing school and knew nothing of the world of jobs or uncertainty. She was truly a "Grand Dame," elegant and cultured. Her "job" was to dress well, run a comfortable house and give exquisite dinner parties---all of which she did beautifully.

The class system was firmly entrenched in Europe and my parents, like the rest of their friends, believed it would be this way forever. And so it was. Until my father died of kidney failure during World War I and our whole world began to change. The war ended when I was five and my mother and I found ourselves considered enemy aliens in a place my family had lived for more than twenty years. We were forced to make the first of many flights from political turmoil when we fled Belgium in the dead of night, leaving all our belongings, money and the beautiful life we had known. Ahead was poverty and uncertainty and we both felt the beginning of the fear that would soon be our constant companion.

My mother chose Germany because she had a sister living in Dusseldorf, so we fled, with only what we could carry of my mother's jewelry. Though we had some heavy gold pieces---chains, bracelets, several good-sized diamond rings---we arrived in Germany penniless. A friend of my mother's helped us sell them and invest the money but we still lived very simply. My mother was terrified of being without money, "a total pauper," and would use it only in extreme emergencies.

We were even too poor to rent a room for fear of using up our nest egg and a kind doctor offered us his waiting room to sleep in during the nights. We stayed with my Aunt Alice and her family during the daytime but when evening came there was no room for us there. So every night we prepared for bed, dressed and walked to the empty office to stretch out on the couches and lumpy chairs. My mother found the transition from Grand Dame to homeless widow and child a difficult one and I often felt her hopelessness and depression. My mother had been born and raised in an affluent Germany with money and privilege and married well (my father owned a prosperous silk factory). Growing up in Germany her family's friends were all wealthy and of high social caste. When she was forced to return to them in poverty, they were all kind but patronizing, something that made it even harder for her. She found it hard to accept that they no longer viewed her as an equal. She still saw herself as un-changed---merely less fortunate than before---not truly lower class. This made working a nightmare for her because she didn't know how to relate to middle class people---their values and needs were totally beyond her comprehension. But we survived on the meager salaries she was able to earn and were eventually able to get one rented room of our own.

It was not until I was ten that some of our Jewish friends found my mother a job more in line with her abilities. She started to work for the B'nai B'rith Lodge, arranging parties---something she was quite good at. Dusseldorf had a beautiful synagogue and the lodgehouse hosted many bar mitzvah, weddings, din-ners and meetings. The city was home to more than five thousand Jews and the lodge was used almost daily. We were given a small apartment and a better salary, which was wonderful. Unlike my mother, I like work-ing class people. Our life began to regain some stabil-ity but my mother was still unhappy. She couldn't deal with the unfortunate turn her life had taken and found fault even with our improved circumstances. We lived there until I was fourteen and then moved to a larger apartment where we were able to rent out one of its rooms.

People have often asked me why the Jews did not leave Germany in 1933. Before '33 we could have left but would not have been able to get visas or work permits in other countries. America, England, France and many others abandoned the Jews and closed their doors. Also, Germany was our homeland. The Jews who had lived there had had their homes and businesses for many generations. They had served in the military and fought many battles for their beloved homeland. My family had emigrated from Spain but had lived in Germany for more than three hundred years. In the early days of Hitler's rise to power, we believed that the anti-Semitism wouldn't last long. Six months, everyone said, and things would be back to normal. It was what we all wanted to believe. Little could we have known that it would be many years, six millions lives lost and countless families shattered and scattered to the ends of the earth, some never to be rejoined. How bitter the realization that they were wrong!

But all of this was before me at this time and fear began to tighten it's grip on me when I started school at the age of six. I was the only Jewish child in my class. I spoke two languages and looked differently from the other children. Children are notoriously hard on anyone different so, of course, they taunted me, threw rocks and insults daily. They were cruel and drove me home crying many a day to our apartment but the worst of this was my teacher. That first day began a six-year period of harassment and cruelty that was like nothing I had ever imagined and only hinted at the horrors to come. Fraulein Dehmeld. The name still makes me shiver to this day. She began each new school year the same way:

"Will any student who is not a Christian please stand up."

I stood up.

Next:

"Will anyone not born in Germany stand up."

I remained standing.

Then:

"Anyone who is an orphan stand up."

I sat down. A brief frown from Fraulein, like I was lying or hiding something.

Then, a sly smile:

"Anyone who is half-orphan, stand up." And I was forced to stand again, alone in front of the class.

"Who is an only child?" I remained standing. Alone again. Always alone.

And so every year began. I learned to hate and fear school. However, something in me refused to yield and my resignation took on the resolution that I would survive. I am convinced that this horrible teacher was in some part responsible for my determination to establish my school and give students a secure and happy learning environment. Years later I would write this vicious woman a letter venting my feelings, telling her how awful she was and that she was a bitch and I hated her. It was a part of my healing process. And a wonderful thing did come out of my years there. I met blond, blue-eyed Margaret Stein, the only Catholic student in our class and we became fast friends. The prejudices we endured forged a strong bond between us. Our bond was a great comfort to me growing up and we shared some terrifying times together, helping each other through experiences that could have destroyed us.

TWO
I Begin to Work

I weathered the years in school until I graduated at eighteen in 1931. The political situation was very bad in Germany. Inflation held us in its grip and the unemployment rate was at its peak. Out of nowhere in 1933, a house painter emerged from Austria, giving speeches that inflamed the passions of German society. He promised better times and a new Germany, forged in iron and racially "pure." Adolf Hitler blamed the Jews for everything and people flocked to his rally. "Kill the Jews, reclaim our Fatherland and create the immortal 'Master Race.' 'Heil Hitler'" was heard everywhere and the Third Reich rose to throw a shadow over all the Jews.

Amidst this turmoil, our daily lives went on. To help with finances, I took a short course in typing and shorthand. I managed to get a job as a secretary and while I was happy to help my mother provide for us, I longed for something more. I had a good voice and wanted to study music. I also had dreams of becoming a physical therapist. But to do either I would have to leave my mother to study and none of my relatives were anxious to see this happen. They loved me but felt my place was with my mother, fulfilling my duties as a daughter. As hard as it was for me to put these dreams aside, I knew I needed to stay with her and so I did. My secretarial career was not a great success to say the least. I moved from job to job, never able to find a situation in which I could realize my full potential.

My first job was with a jeweler in Obercassel who had his store in his home. His wife was the bookkeeper and I made out the tickets for every item. I was not good at this and was constantly in trouble. The jeweler was no help either. All he wanted was for his wife to leave the house to run an errand and make me sit on his lap. I was young, totally inexperienced and terrified of losing my job so finally I did and, of course, his wife chose that moment to return and I was fired on the spot. Next, I worked in a large corporation as a secretary to one of the younger executives. He dictated letters that were badly written and I would rewrite them, something he didn't appreciate but would have tolerated if I had been willing to stay after office hours and allow him to "instruct" me. This instruction, as I was beginning to learn, was me letting him kiss and fondle me which was so frightening. I immediately quit.

In 1930, the depression hit Germany full-force. My mother had inherited from an aunt a nice amount of money that could have made our lives easier, but inflation made the 10,000 Deutshe Reichsmarks almost worthless and again, we had nothing. I remember standing in line to get flour, sugar or butter and finding when I reached the front that the price was four times higher than it had been for the people before me. It was during this period of turmoil when I could get no job because I was a Jew that I sought comfort in my life's avocation of music. I had played the guitar and sung folk songs as young as six. I was encouraged to audition for the voice teacher at the University of Cologne. Since the University was close to home, there was a chance that I might be able to pursue a singing career. I was overjoyed to give up my secretarial work--probably no happier than my employers were to see me go---and try to sing. The teacher was very pleased with my voice, hoping that I could be trained as a liedersinger. My relatives reluctantly gave me their support and I enrolled at the University.

THREE
The Beast Shows Itself

My happiness was short-lived. Every day at school we gathered for an assembly. We were expected to sing "Deutchland, Uber Alles" and greet each other and our teachers with the "seig heil," or "heil Hitler." I could not bring myself to return the salute and say those hated words like the rest of my classmates. It became increasingly difficult for me to hide my Jewish identity. Fear closed on me like an icy grip, choking the joy from my music and becoming so intense that I had to leave school. Temple was one of my refuges and it was there that I met Ernest Tarrasch, the organist who played for our choir (we had both gotten our positions when the temple had to let the Gentiles holding these jobs go). Ernest was a fabulous organist and the most fascinating man I had ever met. I listened to him play for many hours. He also played the piano masterfully and was studying medicine. I fell in love immediately and was overjoyed to find he returned my feelings. We shared our music, the rush of first love and courtship and we shared our fear. Fear of the Nazis, fear that they would come for us in the night as they already had some of our friends. These bonds brought us together in a way that few young people our age could have understood. We loved each other and together we could face the uncertainty of our future with a united front.

In Germany everything had stopped for the Jews. Ernest could not finish his internship or residency there. We knew he would have to leave. We decided to become engaged, taking a chance in not knowing where or when we would be able to live in peace together. Our courtship was a sad one. Jews weren't allowed in restaurants, theatres or movies. It was always better to stay at home because then we didn't have to read the slogans scrawled on the main streets, "Kill the Jews and Stray Dogs." We didn't have to listen to the loud speakers in the larger cities shouting Hitler's poison that Jews were the Evil of the World and must all be eradicated. The messages were clear and cruel and no one will ever convince me that any German could not have known about them.

An Uncle of Ernest's in North America made it possible for him to finish his education at an eye clinic in Vienna. Hitler had not marched through Austria yet and Vienna was still a safe place. I desperately wanted to follow him but could not leave my mother ill and unable to care for herself. We said goodbye, not sure we would ever see each other again.

FOUR

A Trip to Belgium and
A Little Peace With Ernest

At twenty-one I received a notice from the Czechoslovakian government that the part of Austria where my father was born had become Czechoslovakia after WWI and I now had to choose which passport and citizenship I would retain. It was advantageous for me to become a Czech citizen since Hitler had not invaded it yet. Another advantage was that my passport would not have "Jew" stamped on it and I could cross the border more often. I had inherited a small amount of money from my father's brother in Czechoslovakia but if I claimed it, I would have to declare it to the German government. To keep from doing this I had to prove that I had established a domicile in another European country. This led me to a new adventure and a little luck. Some of the last luck I would see for a long time.

To establish a domicile was a very complicated procedure because I had to prove that I had lived in another country for many years and was financially independent. My first thought was to go to Belgium, it was close to Germany and it was, after all, the place I had been born. I was very frightened to go alone and asked my good friend Margaret to go with me. My idea probably seemed silly and vague---find a rabbi and try to get him to help me in any way possible---but it was the only plan I had and I was desperate so we decided on a small town close to the German border called Spa. My mother had spent her honeymoon there and what little she had told me of the town sounded lovely. We had no trouble getting across the border on the train since Margaret was a Gentile and I was technically a Czechoslovakian citizen.

On the train that took us to Spa, we were only allowed to bring five German marks each which was about the equivalent of $2.00. Spa was much smaller than I'd anticipated and there was no rabbi there. We were worried, but able to find a room over a stable for a mark a night and too scared to eat for fear of running out of money. We racked our brains...what to do next? I had the idea to go to the nearest police station and ask for the highest ranking officer and hope that he could give us some advice. Our hearts threatening to jump out of our chests, we must have been flushed and stammering, excited and frightened at the same time. We thought surely all of the other officers would stare but surprisingly, they didn't give us a second look. Monsieur Niki, the officer in charge must have been visited by several flushed and stammering young ladies on a regular basis. I knew that any conversation we had would have to be in French, but my French was quite rusty. We were led into Monsieur's office and found a distinguished man in his sixties, well-preserved and friendly, shaking our hands and saying, "oh, la blonde et la noire" the blonde and the brunette with a twinkle in his eye.

Monsieur Niki made it clear that whatever favor we desired, it could wait until we had "met" socially. He suggested dinner that very night and "la blonde et la noire" agreed instantly---a free meal and still a chance to plead my case. We couldn't refuse. In the forest surrounding the town there was a little restaurant where a married man could safely entertain us, but we were instructed to meet him at the bus station, enter the bus when he did and get off when he got off, then follow him. We were game and bravely followed him onto the bus. We had no money, of course, to buy our two tickets which he courteously took care of by buying three tickets and dropping two of them on the floor for us to retrieve when no one was looking.

The restaurant was a very nice place and conversation was slow but charming. It had been a long day and we were grateful to be eating a good dinner and relaxing instead of walking the streets searching for help. We gobbled our food so quickly that I'm sure he knew we were desperate for his help. He didn't mention it though, and asked us to meet him again the following evening at a hotel around seven o'clock. We agreed and he embraced us and said goodnight when we were ready to leave. This new opportunity meant we would have to stay another day or two so we kept the room over the stable. The next day, with lighter hearts and hope that Monsieur Niki would help us, we did a little sightseeing, feeling like normal tourists, carefree and enjoying the moment---something I needed very badly. We drank coffee or water, laughing and working our way toward the hotel where we would meet our new friend. We arrived at seven and asked for Monsieur Niki in room 12. As scared as we were, when we opened the door to the room and saw nothing but a bed, a nightstand and another bed, we burst out laughing, visualizing Monsieur Niki hopping from bed to bed! I was to share a bed with him as the first "victim," and he was very kind. I broke down and cried in his arms, telling him the truth about why we were there. He was understanding and sympathetic and took us both out to dinner and made arrangements to see us in his office the next day. He took care of everything. He saved my life when he stamped on my passport that I had been living in Belgium. Many years later when I was married and living with Ernest in Springfield, surrounded by my loving family, I wrote to him, thanking him for his kindness. He sent my husband a wonderful letter, congratulating him for "marrying such a brave girl."

By establishing my residency in Belgium I could now go back to Germany secure in the knowledge that I did not have to declare my inheritance. I could never thank Margaret enough for those amazing three days in Belgium; I would never have had the courage to go alone.

I was unable to work in Germany or go to school. I began to feel that I was being followed by the Nazis. It was very unsettling and I decided to go to Vienna to visit Ernest. It was a wonderful time for us. We were both in love and so happy to be together. We rented a single room and lived together as man and wife. We have laughed about it many times, how lucky we were that I didn't become pregnant. I remember that I thought many times how different things would have been if I had only myself to consider, not my mother and I. With only myself to consider my life might have been very different. But even then, my course was set. My journey through fear was only beginning.

We spent hours exploring Vienna, the beautiful gardens, walking in the park, sitting in cabarets, holding hands. With hardly any money we usually had to keep our "imbibing" to a glass of wine each as we sat at the long tables in the little "wein stuben" where we felt the most at home. There were also small, inexpensive theaters where we watched light comedies and tried to forget our worries, reveling in the fact that we were together. We lived as if there were no tomorrow---something all Jews had begun to face everyday. Overshadowing our love and happiness, of course, was the relentless question of when the Nazis would invade Austria---knowing that when they did, Ernest and I would never see each other again.

All too soon I received news from my Aunt Alice that it was essential for me to return to Germany to care for my mother whose heart problems had worsened. So with a heavy heart, I left Ernest behind and returned to Hitler's new Germany.

FIVE
The Beast Roars and Knocks at Our Door and Then England Beckons

My mother and I were living in Dusseldorf where we had a small apartment on the third floor. Mother could barely climb those stairs, stopping to rest on each landing, red-faced, having difficulty getting her breath every time. There were about five doctors left to treat thousands of Jews, so medical treatment was almost impossible to get. And even if we could have found a doctor, no Jews were allowed in any hospital except one Catholic facility that could only reserve three rooms to house the most critically ill. There was no one to care for my mother but me and the Catholic Sisters who stopped by once or twice a week to help me bathe her, a great service, considering they could have been reported to the Nazis and punished for helping a Jew.

The Nazis started to follow me in earnest now---I never really knew why---Jews were being rounded up every day but the Nazis had so far left me alone because of my Czechoslovakian passport. My mother implored me to leave her, to get out while I could---that she feared for me here. And in my heart I knew I could never leave her to the mercy of the Third Reich and its henchmen; but I was afraid and I wanted so much to go. The conflict and guilt tortured me long after her death, long into the terrible dark night that was Germany under Hitler.

The incidents were too many to count. At three o'clock in the morning two young Nazis, hardly more than seventeen, knocked on our door, armed with guns and looking for jewelry or money in our three-room apartment. We were too afraid to keep anything valuable at home of course, but they dragged us from our beds anyway, pinning us against the wall and throwing everything from our drawers to the floor, tearing the closets apart, laughing while we froze in terror. This went on for weeks, over and over. Once my mother passed out and fell to the floor, moaning with pain. I begged them to let me bring her some water but they forced me to watch her cry out , helpless and afraid. These horrible little visits made mother's heart worse and worse. I knew that I had to get out of Germany soon but there was no way I could have taken my mother. The decision had to be made. But could I leave the one person I loved most in the world, the one person who had given me all she could for my whole life and who now needed me more than ever? The reality of what I had to do was almost more than I could bear and whatever I did, the consequences would be devastating for both of us, leaving me scarred and guilt-ridden and my mother to face her illness and fear alone. Something had to be done.

Once again, my family ties opened a door for me. My cousin, Gerda Selo was a dentist in England in 1933--no mean feat, since the English were not fond of women in any man's profession, but particularly not the medical arts. She had struggled to make a living for years but refused to give up and had managed to keep her practice going. She knew I needed to leave Germany and understood my mother's health would force her to stay. She offered me a place to stay, a job and asked her sister in Dusseldorf with a family of five children to take care of my mother for a short time. I made the decision to go, knowing they would take good care of mother but our parting was difficult. She was terrified for me to leave her. In her heart she wanted me to be safe but couldn't get past her fear of abandonment. But I had made up my mind to try to make a place for myself and hope my mother could hold out until I could get her out also.

I left for England with the wording on my visa stating, "Allowed to enter England without permission to work, either paid or unpaid." This rule was the same in every European country because unemployment was high and jobs were not to be given to foreigners; however, shortly after I arrived Gerda told me she had a non-paying job with room and board for me with a wealthy older lady. I would be her companion if she went out dancing, walking, shopping or whatever she wished and in return I would have a beautiful room overlooking the ocean and best of all---I didn't have to do any housework.

She was a very proper English lady and ran a very proper English household. I was instructed that I was to say nothing that might be shocking to the Lady's sensibilities---which seemed to be just about everything in the normal world. I had to be very careful and watch how I worded even the most innocent of comments. For example, the only illness I could refer to or discuss was "indigestion." If my arms or legs or any other part of my body hurt, it was "indigestion." She was of the highest English caste and had many peculiarities and odd beliefs for someone who insisted on everything being so incredibly proper. Like many other rich English of the time, she considered herself a spiritualist and spoke regularly with her husband, which wouldn't have been so odd if he had not been two years deceased. Believing that her dead husband's soul returned to earth periodically, she opened her bedroom window each night at eleven o'clock and welcomed his spirit in for a little chat. Not that this would have been any of my concern, except our bedrooms shared a wall and I couldn't help but hear her conversations with him. They lasted exactly one hour and she brought him up to date on her day and business decisions, etc. I don't remember a male voice responding, but at midnight I would hear her open her window, bid him goodnight and go to sleep. At first it didn't bother me but after a while I couldn't sleep until I heard her escort him out her window and say goodnight.

As if this wasn't odd enough, she made me attend her Spiritualist's Church. The minister was very charming and made everyone comfortable and greeted most of the members with "Dear Madame, I spoke to your husband last night and he is fine and carrying the umbrella you gave him for his last birthday." Everybody would then smile and feel much better. At the time, he seemed quite nice and concerned, but now I think perhaps he had less charitable motives.

For two months everything went well and then trouble arrived in the form of the woman's young son who was studying at Oxford and home on a short vacation. Again, she warned me strenuously not to speak of any body parts. The son arrived late at night and I didn't meet him until the next morning at breakfast. When the butler rang the bell in the morning I was a few minutes late in coming down to the table. Summoning up the best Shakespearean English I could remember, I blurted out "I am so sorry to be late, I was cleaning my chamber." The young man, thinking I was referring to my chamber pot, rolled on the floor laughing. The Lady was horrified and fired me on the spot for using such foul language. I didn't lose all that much, since she didn't pay me anything but I had to return to my cousin's house.

I found a job in a girl's boarding house teaching German and French but the police found out I was working and ordered me out of England in forty-eight hours. With help from friends I was able to buy a ticket to Belgium where I immediately found a job as a waitress. I had worked for about three weeks when the police again found me and shipped me directly back to England to Cousin Gerda. And there I found what I had feared most all along. A letter waited for me that said I needed to return to Germany. My mother was dying.

SIX
The Beast Revealed and My Flight

Retuning to Germany I found my mother in a terrible state. I found a way to get her admitted to the Catholic hospital and got her into the ambulance but she was too sick and tired to go on and died before we reached the hospital. I was horrified to realize that my first feeling was relief. Relief that she wouldn't have to suffer anymore. Relief that she would not have to face the final crumbling of our life in Germany but worst of all---relief that I could leave Germany now. I loved her very much but the time had come for me to say goodbye and run for my life.

I remember little of the funeral. I was the only one who attended and my mind was already planning how I could leave the country for the last time. My life was in danger and there was no time for grief or to deal with the guilt and torment I felt at losing my only parent. An odd thought went through my mind...the Fraulein from my school would be so pleased at last---I was finally an orphan. My mother was buried as Meta Kaff in 1935 in Dusseldorf when I was twenty-two years old.

I applied for an exit visa which was still possible since I was not a German citizen and it was granted. I started to pack my belongings under the watchful glare of three Nazis. They took everything I had left except for a small suitcase with one change of clothes, a toothbrush and five Deutsche Marks. I did not return to the cemetery. I left for England the next day. I was sitting comfortably in the train car, anxious to have the border behind me, certain that I would make it since Hitler had not yet taken Czechoslovakia. The two-hour ride from Dusseldorf to Aachen near the Belgium border was like a nightmare for me. My head was pounding, my palms clammy and my stomach was a stone.

We arrived at the border crossing and stopped while two Nazis with german shepherd dogs went through the train. They stopped in front of me, raking me over with their eyes and told me to get up and follow them. With a sinking heart I was taken to a little room where they left me with two huge female Nazis with guns. They treated me roughly, demanding that I undress so that they could search my body for hidden jewelry or valuables. They were lesbians and assaulted me for over two hours with torture, insults and repeated forcible rapes. Dazed and miserable I dressed as they demanded before kicking me out of the office leaving me to stumble into the first rail-car I could find. It was a boxcar full of hay and I dropped onto it and mercifully passed out. When I came to I had crossed the

German border, was in Belgium, and I was free.

I remember very little about that time. My mother's death, the shock of my assault, my physical pain made it all a blur but I do remember crawling out of the car at the first stop and asking for the train master. I told him my story, showed him my ticket to England and with the help of several people I was able to cross the channel. I arrived in Southhampton and Gerda picked me up and took me to Bournemouth where she lived. I was hardly able to speak or eat so she took me to a doctor who diagnosed my case as hysterical amnesia. I was put on a liquid diet for several weeks and Cousin Gerda nursed me back to health. It was during this time I realized that America was probably my only chance for a future now. I had only immigrated to England and had no work visa so I could not stay there long.

I had not seen Ernest Tarrasch for two years but we had kept in touch through mutual friends. He had made his way to America and gotten an internship in Colorado Springs. I was delighted for him. He had worked so hard, and I was very proud. With him in America, I realized that to have a future with him I would have to make my way there too which was very difficult at the time. In order for me to get into the United States the regulations stated that someone must sponsor me and furnish an affidavit that could guarantee my living expenses for five years. The affidavit giver must have a well-paying job and money in the bank. It was far from the time that Ernest could provide this for me so I would have to bide my time. I remember thinking that President Roosevelt made immigration for Jews very difficult if not impossible. I resigned myself to the fact that I would have to find work in England again. I had talked to the American Consulate and they rudely told me I would never get there. I was crushed and returned to Bournemouth.

This time I found a job in a Jewish hotel. They asked about my experience and I assured them I had done this job before. I told them about my life, admitting that I could only work at night when the police would be less likely to find me. They rewarded my honesty with total acceptance and embraced me. They said they would hide me from the police and do all that they could to help me. The people were wonderful but very strange. They were also tremendously overweight. The wife's sister also worked at the hotel and she must have weighed three hundred and fifty pounds on a light day. I was very small and I'm sure we made a very odd picture but they couldn't have been kinder and shielded me from everything they could. They were also very understanding with my mistakes. My first night was so difficult. There was a lot to do and the orders came continually. "Fraulein, please send coffee to my room at ten o'clock," Fraulein, please draw my bath water at ten thirty," Fraulein, please bring the newspaper to room 100," Please knock on my door at five a.m. so that I can let Miss Brown out." It went on and on. One night I forgot to turn off the bath water and it flooded the second floor. I cried so hard that all of the guests helped me mop the floor. They all knew I needed the job and that I was a Jewish refugee. I got little money but the tips were generous. I worked in the mornings for a few hours emptying and cleaning chamber pots which was not my favorite job. One morning I even fell with one of them but thankfully, no one saw me!

One night a nice looking young man came rather late to the hotel and we talked for a long time before he went to his room. He asked me to go dancing the next evening and I was delighted because he was so handsome and I had been so sad for such a long time. The party was wonderful and I danced every dance with him. Afterwards we walked by the sea where he showed me a big stone which was placed in the sand. I was feeling very gay, excited by the night and flushed from dancing. He pointed at the stone and said "Five days ago I buried my dog here. I loved him so. Now I

am going to dig him up and see what he looks like."
My high spirits were immediately doused and I shud-
dered, telling him I wasn't feeling well and wanted to
go back. We walked the long way back without a word
between us which was fine with me. He left me at the
hotel and thankfully, I never saw him again.

Not to be dissuaded I accepted another date with
a man who was very shy. We met many times to walk
in the public gardens. On one of these walks he suddenly turned his face toward mine and kissed me. After he recovered, he said, "I have never kissed a woman
in the park." He blushed and I took his hand as we
walked on quietly. He was very sweet but our friendship didn't last too long. He was too boring. Or maybe
he just wasn't my Ernest.

I wrote to Ernest about how desperate I was to
join him. I had already waited two years on my papers. It seemed that no one was going to be able to
help me, but fate stepped in again and changed my
life. Ernest had gone to a party with other physicians
and everybody drank too much and just generally had
a good time. One of the doctors had turned to him
suddenly and asked him if he had a girlfriend. Ernest
told him about me and my dilemma and one of the
other doctors overheard the conversation. He declared
loudly that he would be the affidavit giver! Fearing he

would not remember, Ernest went to see him the next day to remind him of his offer. Not wanting to go back on his word after speaking up so loudly and so publicly, the doctor started the process. Many papers had to be signed---much of what we now call "red tape"---but after weeks I heard that Ernest had co-signed the affidavit and had to declare that we would be married five days after my arrival. In the meantime I had to keep working in England until my paperwork came through which took another six months.

When the moment finally came, I withdrew the money I had gone through so much to protect from the Germans and purchased my ticket to America. I was happy, excited, scared---to be married in five days under the conditions of my secured visa was both a blessing and a curse. A strange land was a frightening thought and I had not seen Ernest in two and a half years. We both had most certainly changed. When we had been together in Vienna I was still a clinging vine, fearful of the Nazis, fearful of losing my mother, afraid all the time. During the years we'd been apart, I had become stronger and more independent---a woman Ernest didn't really know. How could I know if he would want this new woman? The years of independence were suddenly not enough to hold back this new kind of fear.

SEVEN
Bon Voyage

Good and faithful friend that she had been, Cousin Gerda took me to Southhampton where I boarded the Aquatania, bound for New York.She had helped me, healed me after the Nazi ordeal and saved me many times. I was determined to start a new life in America but it meant that again, I would have to leave someone I loved behind. Our parting was very emotional as she wished me well. In many ways, when I had lost my mother and been all alone, she had replaced her as well as she could. I would miss her.

The Aquatania was an enormous luxury liner with three thousand passengers on board. After I was shown to my cabin, my courage and resolve drained right our of me. The fear of my new life washed over me, a flood of doubt and uncertainty, of missing the life I had made in England---my only home since Germany. I stayed for two or three days in my cabin without leaving. I was all alone, on my way to a new land that I thought would be full of "cowboys" and "Indians," and full of strangers---again. After I regained my resolve to meet this new life head on, I ventured out of my cabin and began talking to people. I discovered that hundreds of the other passengers were also Jewish immigrants. They also had my same fear of the unknown. We had all suffered so much under Hitler and had a hard time believing that it could really be over. Before the boat docked I had made many friends, bonded with these people in a way that was hard to describe to someone who has not shared such a traumatic experience and shared it with so many others. I had at least three marriage proposals from men who were also afraid to start their new life alone. We all shared a powerful fear that had been our constant companion for so long that we were afraid to believe in the future again. The closeness we all shared was very special, a sense of having been brought together at that time and place by the hand of fate.

EIGHT
The Beautiful America: Colorado Springs

If life in England had conditioned me to live in fear, immersion in my new life and American culture was a different kind of the same thing in a way. There were so many unknowns and I was still crippled by the fear that had dominated me for most of my life. I was greeted in New York by friends of Ernest's, an older man who had lost his wife to the concentration camps, a physician, Dr. Loevenstein. He was very good and kind to me but during the night of my stay in his home he begged me not to leave and to become his wife. This may sound inappropriate, but you must understand that all Jews who had lived in Germany, had our homes, families and property ripped away by the Nazis were insecure---when we met other Jews who shared our experience we had a tendency to bond with them very quickly. He was lonely, knew I understood his pain, the indescribable agony of what the Nazis did to so many of us. He didn't want to stay alone and vulnerable. It was hard to lose this even in a new land where things were different. I refused him gently and got on another train---this time to take me to Colorado Springs and Ernest---and marriage. I had no fingernails left by the time I got there. I was terrified. I fell into his arms, but we both could feel the time between us and the different people we had become. We only had three days left before we had to get married so there was little time to think or consider anything else. Also, I had come from sea level in England all the way up to the mountains of Colorado---I was exhausted and sick but there was no time to waste.

Ernest was a resident physician at the Printers Home in Colorado Springs and had to return to work soon so we found the rabbi who was to marry us. We had no money for a wedding dress but by chance I fit into the gown that the rabbi's wife had worn so all we had to buy was a veil---my entire trousseau! I was still sick and scared during the ceremony. I wondered who would come to the wedding of a poor, terrified little refugee girl in a borrowed dress, but, lo and behold, the temple was filled to capacity. It was the first Jewish wedding in seven years there and it was wonderful to see so many gathering to celebrate with someone they didn't even know. But though the wedding was lovely, we looked at each other, knowing the road ahead was going to be difficult. We didn't know if we would make it---there are never any guarantees---but the odds were against us. We fought like cats and dogs all during our honeymoon, wondering if our marriage would last a month. Returning to our Colorado Springs home, I felt sluggish and depressed.

I went to many doctors who diagnosed a nervous stomach disorder and gave me pills and new diets. Three months passed and I was still very sick, very fearful of everything around me and very unhappy. We lived in a one room apartment and Ernest continued his residency at Printers. He was only able to come home once a week and a life that had been uncertain but full of excitement and change seemed empty and dull. Maybe I was so afraid still that I couldn't accept anything else. Maybe I couldn't let myself be happy because the guilt of leaving my mother when she had been ill and being with her only briefly when she died and leaving Germany so quickly afterward wouldn't let me rest or relax into my new life. I don't know but I was unhappy and still afraid. I didn't know anyone in town and cried most of the time. Ernest felt sorry for me and brought me a little dog to keep me company. It became my constant companion, someone to tell all my troubles to, a friend at last. After three months had passed, a physician's wife came to visit me. she told me that she wanted to be honest with me---I looked terrible and she was sure I was pregnant. I called Ernest and told him what she had said. He became angry and told me he would order a "rabbit test" to prove me wrong. Ten days later he called and tenderly asked how I felt and told me that he was sorry to have been angry with me---and that I was pregnant. I was hysterical. I wasn't ready for a child. I hadn't even adjusted to being married yet. I wasn't over all my dreadful experiences---I missed my mother and again, I was afraid---still. I pleaded with Ernest to go to an abortionist with me. He knew how devastated I was and we went together. The office was filthy and we were afraid to stay. Maybe that settled in my mind that I should put my faith in the future and try to bring a new life into the world. Through the next months I began to feel better and be happier---I looked forward to our child---the person who would share my life for many years to come. This child would be named Eleanor after Eleanor Roosevelt, a woman I admired for being strong-willed and independent in a turbulent time.

Though happier, I was plagued by many phobias during my pregnancy. Once I went to a fire sale at Penney's that I had seen advertised. I wanted to buy something for my baby and was the first one in line waiting for the store to open. After half an hour I looked back and saw the people behind me and panicked. It reminded me of the Nazis putting a sign on the outside of a very famous delicatessen that was owned by Jews that read, "No one is allowed to enter this store." I had refused to be daunted by this and went in anyway but was so afraid that I could barely tell them what I wanted. I realized I couldn't get through the crowd to leave the store, and I panicked and could not move. There were some decent Gentiles in Germany, and one of them, a policeman on the scene led me gently through the crowd to his car and took me home. Why I rashly tried to be brave was a mystery--I just knew I wanted to stand up to the oppression and fear we all lived with daily. The incident reminded me of all my paralyzing fears and would surface many times in the years to come. It all came rushing back as I saw the crowd at Penneys and I fainted. I was taken to a hospital where I stayed for a few days until I felt better. But even after recovering, I could barely stand to be left alone, something common with survivors of the Nazi tyranny. I couldn't cross the street. When I went into a department store I could only stay on the ground floor---afraid to use either the elevator or the stairs. I had to be somewhere with an easy escape route---I was still running away.

Another time I tried to get a permanent at a beauty shop. At this time this process required the patron to be hooked up to a machine by the hair. When I felt myself unable to move away I screamed and passed out. They rushed me to the hospital where they gave me drugs and I stayed another few days---the incidents seemed to increase as the birth of my daughter drew nearer. The only solace I could find was that after her birth, I wouldn't have to be alone anymore.

After a long and difficult pregnancy, my Eleanor was born. My fears threatened to overwhelm me again---fear for this child in a world that I was afraid to face---that I was sure could only hold despair or danger. I had to learn to curb these fears for the love of this child. A short time after her birth I found I was pregnant again and this time I handled it much better. I was able to feel the joy of bringing a child into the world where a loving mother, father and doting baby sister awaited it. My son Tony was born to his delighted sister Eleanor and our household lightened up immediately. The children became fast friends for life. They never fought and Eleanor protected him at all times. If one of us tried to discipline Tony she would immediately get between us and stretch out her arms, refusing to budge until we were no longer angry. They constantly played the game of 'brother and sister." They didn't need anyone else. Their personalities were totally opposite---Eleanor quiet and Tony boisterous, but there could never have been a stronger bond between them.

In order to provide for his new family Ernest had many strange jobs to supplement our income. He worked at Penney's selling shoes during the Christmas season and then he found work in a pea shed, selling peas. During the summer he worked, the only white man in a Mexican crew, hauling hundred-pound sacks of potatoes in the freight yards. It took a heavy physical toll on him.

When Eleanor was a year old, we heard that Ernest's father would be coming to live with us so we began the hunt for a larger apartment that we could afford. Papa Tarrasch had immigrated to Holland and since Hitler took over there shortly afterwards, he had immediately had to make plans to leave and we were his only avenue. He had lost his wife and was alone, something I understood very well, so we took him in. The story of his arrival in the United States and becoming a citizen is a treasured memory.

Papa had caught the last boat from Europe before WWII. He had been in prison and we were so worried about him. He was robbed of everything he had ever owned and had left his homeland and his friends---not an easy adjustment for a seventy-year-old man. We had not seen him for years and expected a pathetic, broken old man. Not Papa Tarrasch! He looked good and as spry as ever. He had been on the ocean twenty-two days with five hundred other passengers. Because of the war, the big ocean liners traveled only at night. While others aboard ship were panic stricken, Papa found the trip fascinating. He was thrilled just to be alive and to have the opportunity to spend the rest of his life in a free country. He was looking forward to a new life, regardless of his age and the fact that he could not speak one word of English. We had feared he would be lonely and isolated. Not Papa! He knew how to make friends and was determined to make the best of the second chance God had offered him. His eyes sparkled with inner light and strength and people flocked around him. The ladies noticed him, charmed by his European gentility and courteous ways. When people spoke to him, he tipped his hat and smiled, eager to shake their hands. No matter what they told him, he responded "Oh fine!"

Papa was penniless when he came here and for the first time in his life he was dependent on his children. I cannot recall that he ever complained, doing everything in his power to make our life easier. While Ernest and I worked he took care of his grandchildren. European men were not very familiar with babies' routines, diapers and such, but he struggled valiantly to learn and was a reliable and entertaining nursemaid.

For years we lived in perfect harmony with Papa

until he decided he must become an American citizen. We tried to talk him out of this notion, explaining how difficult the examination was, that he would have to learn American history, pass oral and written tests which would be virtually impossible with his limited English, but he refused to listen. When we tried to forget about it, he asked some of our friends to help him fill out his application papers. Many were young students who seemed delighted to be of assistance. Papa had a great deal of trouble retaining all the facts, dates and names but his iron determination prevailed and he kept at it.

When a letter arrived telling Papa to appear at the courthouse in three days for his examination, he panicked. He knew he had not learned enough and felt he could not pass the test. By this time we all felt that we could not let him down after all his hard work and determination. We knew we had to help him fulfill this dream. It was almost a whole community project. Family and friends came in droves to work with him, quizzing him, shouting the questions because of his failing hearing. I doubted he could understand most of what we were saying but his standard response was, "Oh yes, I understand!" Finally it was time and we went to the courthouse with him.

The examiner entered the courtroom and , as if

fate had wanted it that way, the examiner was an old man also. He looked at Papa and asked him his name. Papa understood and answered correctly, "My name is Martin Tarrasch."

The examiner came closer and apparently, he too, was a little hard of hearing. "Do you speak English?"

Papa looked nervously at his witnesses. When they nodded, he said, "Oh yes."

The examiner's eyes rested on Papa. He probably noticed how pale Papa was and how his hands trembled. He asked Papa one more question. "Do you like freedom?"

Papa knew the answer to this. His eyes firmly on the examiner, he said
"Oh yes.!" And Papa became a citizen

He lived with us for thirteen years until he passed away, and in this time became the father I had lost. I loved him dearly. He was also a great help to me with my phobias. He never let me go anywhere alone and from that time on I felt more at ease. My phobias vastly improved when he came to us but I still had to cling to my father-in-law and children, especially Eleanor, to keep myself together.

After Ernest's term of residency ended, he could not stay at Printers because he could not be board certified to practice until he became an American citizen.

To do that he had to have lived in the states for six years. He had to move on. By chance, he heard of a position which had opened up for a piano teacher in Monta Vista, Colorado. The teacher there had left thirty or forty students and so Ernest accepted this job and we continued our exodus to the mountains. Since we had very little money, we rented an old truck, loaded our meager belongings and hired a driver to get us to Monta Vista. We followed in case anything should fall off. Thank heavens Ernest had two professions. The most precious possession we had was Ernest's piano, the rest of our belongings being baggage and old furniture.

NINE
Monta Vista

Someone found us an apartment and we were glad to have the exhausting trip behind us. The apartment was too small and with the money friends had given us for our journey, we rented a house. There was no central heating, only a wood stove which went out every time I looked at it. The cook stove was also wood burning and my life in the new town started with enormous frustrations. Ernest started classes shortly after we left which left me alone with Papa, two little children and a dog. Ernest gave two concerts and was asked to be the organist at the Methodist church which brought in a little extra money, but I had to go to work and took a job as a cook in a nearby hospital. I rose every morning at five and fixed breakfast for the patients and staff---through rain, sleet, snow or sunshine. I carried Eleanor with me while Papa stayed with Tony.

I had never done this kind of work before and it was hard for me but I was known for being a very good cook. At eight o'clock the bus picked up Eleanor for the daycare center and when I finished my work I walked back home. Once I came home to find Papa in great need of help---Tony's diaper needed changing!

We stayed there for two years and became a real

curiosity to the townspeople---the only Jewish family they had ever seen. The time drew nearer for Ernest to try for his citizenship papers. An examiner came from Alamosa, the nearest large town, to examine Ernest. The exam lasted at least two hours---a procedure that usually lasts twenty minutes. I found out later that the examiner was fascinated with Ernest's intellect and his knowledge of American history. They spent most of the time, while we were anxiously awaiting news of whether Ernest had passed or not, discussing many things---mostly unrelated to the exam.

After two weeks Ernest received his citizenship papers. Now he could try to pass the State Medical Board to earn his certification so that he could practice medicine in America. Colorado's Boards were notoriously difficult so Ernest did some research and decided to try for his certification in Missouri, usually an easier test. He studied for months and left for Jefferson City to take the exam. Now another waiting game began but life had to continue while we were waiting to know if he would receive his certification.

By the time he left for Missouri, I was in pretty bad shape. I had had many problems with the altitude and was perpetually ill. We had been on such a tight budget that none of us had new clothes, my hair hadn't been cut in two years and I had grown despondent again. I had a cousin living in Findley, Ohio, who was a physician and I called him to ask for help. He immediately invited the children and me to stay with him while Ernest was in Jefferson City. Papa went to visit friends in New York and so we left for Ohio.

The first thing my wonderful cousin and his family did for us when we arrived was to take us all to buy new clothes and send me to the beauty shop. We actually got to enjoy a vacation of sorts while we were there and stayed longer than we had planned. In the meantime, Ernest wrote that he was sure he hadn't passed the exam. My cousin and his wife had taken very good care of us in Ohio. I had gained weight and looked more like myself and the children had blossomed. My attitude was much better and I realized that Ernest needed us to return Monta Vista to make some decisions about where to go next. I felt stronger and ready to tackle my life again.

A picture of the house I was born in, taken in Brussels in 1959.

Bettina at three and a half years old

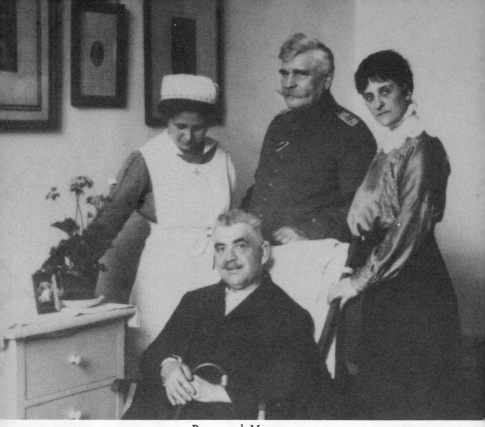

Papa and Mama

Meta Hedvig Kaff, outdoor
restaurant by the Rhine

Sophie Kramer

A Cherished Little Princess

Henrich, Bettina and Meta Kaff, 1915

Papa Tarrasch, approx. 1930

Ernest as a boy.

Ena, Blankenberghe, 1926

Brussels, 1926

Dusseldorf, 1930

Dusseldorf, 1930.

Fish Market in Altona,1937.
Hamburg, 1937.

Another locomotive, 1932. Ernest loved locomotives
Dusseldorf, 1930.   Dusseldorf, 1930.

Berlin, friends 1930

Ernest Tarrasch, 1932.

Ena, in England, 1937.   An old Girl Friend of Ernest's

Ena and Ernest in Vienna, 1936.

Apartment house where Ena and her mother
lived was bombed during the war, 1965.

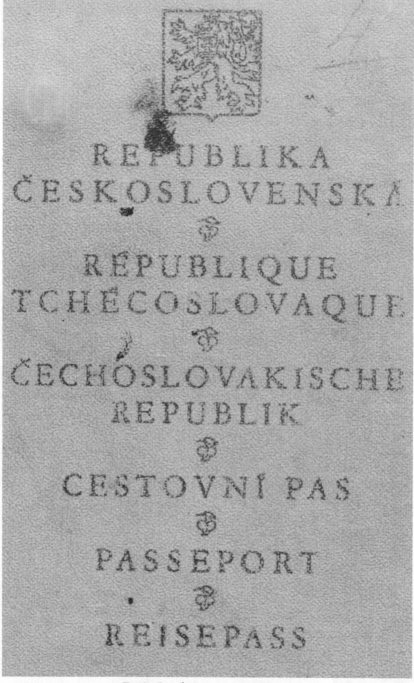

REPUBLIKA
ČESKOSLOVENSKÁ

RÉPUBLIQUE
TCHÉCOSLOVAQUE

ČECHOSLOVAKISCHE
REPUBLIK

CESTOVNÍ PAS

PASSEPORT

REISEPASS

Ena's Czech Passport, 1925.

Ena's immigration visa to England 1938.

The stamped visa shows that Ena is not permitted to work, paid or unpaid, Jews could go to other countries but not earn a living.

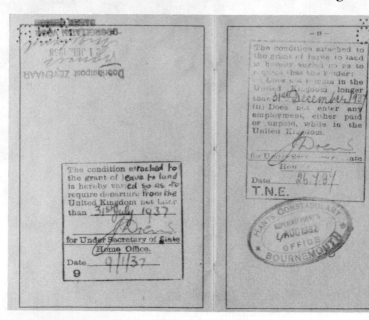

Mr. and Mrs. Ernest Tarrasch, Sept. 18, 1938,
Colorado Springs, USA

The bride and groom, the Rabbi and his wife and our best man, Dr. Lee Briskman

Eleanor is born in Colorado Springs, 1939.

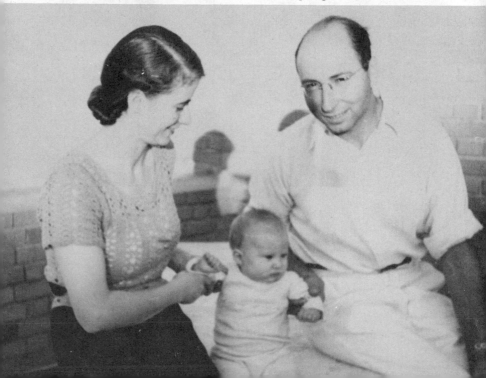

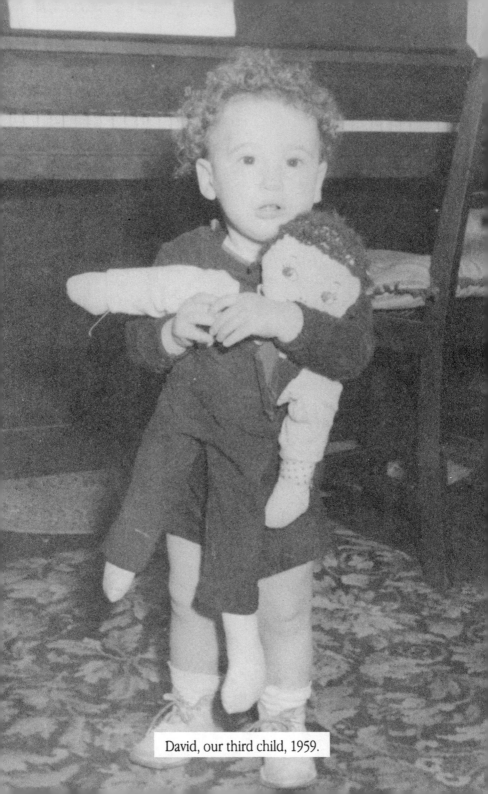

David, our third child, 1959.

Papa and Tony, 1946.   Papa and David, 1948.

Our first home on Calhoun Street

Eleanor, David and Tony.

Rabbi Ernest Jacobs Sunday school class, 1955. The rabbi taught here for 25 years. Eleanor and Tony in the fourth row and David in the second.

Joy and Mimi.

Race car built by Tony for a
Boys Club event.

Eleanor's Quartet.

Our family orchestra.

Central High School, Eleanor in the drum corps.

Mimi.

David holding the Torah at his daughter Allison's batmitzvo. The Torah is handed down from each generation and never leaves the temple.

כבד את לא תהסד

Ena's Preschool Days.

A Maypole Dance.

Preschool
Chanukah
celebration.

Our Family's Chanukah celebration.

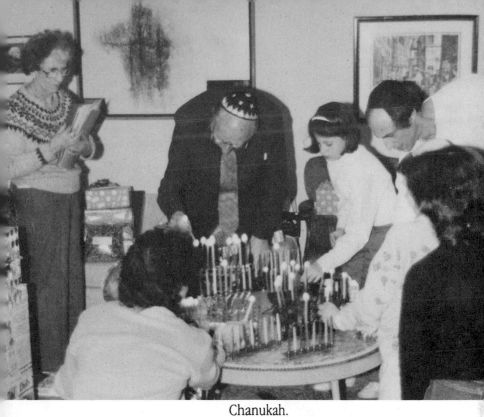
Chanukah.

Joy with the
Chanukah garment.

Chanukah.

One of our Family Portraits.
Ena and Cousin Gerda, Bournemouth, 1959.

Our family in the temple at Chanukah.
Eleanor, Mimi, and the twins, Joel and Trevor, March, 1989.

Huio NGO, our first Vietnamese refugee with me and his natural mother.

The Tarrasch Extended Family. "I am the beginning of all this big family!"
The Tarrasch Extended Family.

The first twins ever born in our family, 1988

Ernie and Ena with Ann and Jim Chen. Ann lived with the Tarrasch's for three years before the wedding.

TEN
We Find Our Haven in Springfield Missouri

In 1944 hospitals all over the country were desperate for doctors, the shortage created by the fact
that many of them had been drafted into service in
WWII. This made it possible for Ernest to apply for a
job without his certification which we did. Pueblo,
Colorado had a state mental hospital which was interested in interviewing Ernest. Anxiously, we drove to
the interview and when Ernest got out of the car we
noticed a huge hole in the back of his pants---the worn
fabric of his "best pants" had just given way. We pooled
our money and went to Penney's and found a pair that
we could afford and sent him off to the interview with
high hopes. He got the job for the duration of the war
and since we were a family, they located a beautiful
home several miles away for us to live in while he
worked there. It had once been used as a patient care
facility and was located in a beautiful park. His salary
was good and we were entitled to free food and rent!
We were delighted and signed the contract right away
and went home to Monta Vista to pack our meager
belongings.

Finishing up with loading the car, I suggested we
stop and check the mail. He went into the post office

and returned, white as a sheet. Fearing something dreadful had happened I asked him if someone had died. He answered "No, it is only that I have passed my state board examination. I am certified to practice but I am committed to working in a state mental hospital for the duration of the war." So Ernest, Papa, the children and I headed for Pueblo and another new home.

Things were going smoothly but my fears, never far beneath the surface, began to make me worry that if something happened to Ernest I would be unable to make a living. I could not go to college because it was too expensive but we could manage to afford a beauty school. I went in the mornings and the children went to preschool. After a year, I passed my Cosmetology Board Examination with flying colors and the owners of the beauty school asked me to take additional training to become an instructor. I did this and my fears began to subside a little. My self-confidence drove my fears back into the shadows.

Just as I became more confident working outside the home, Ernest began to feel that I was neglecting our home and children---and him also. I guess he was flexing his "male chauvinist muscles" a little but I stood my ground. I wanted and needed a profession also. This conflict led to troubles in our relationship. Looking back, it seems ironic that we had lived relatively well through so many traumas and hardships in our marriage and now that we were much more comfortable, our marriage was falling apart. We talked about divorce. Papa assured me that he wished to go wherever I went, leaving his son if necessary.

We made an appointment with an elderly Jewish divorce lawyer in Chicago who had been recommended by friends. I don't know quite what we expected, but he began by asking Ernest if I was a good wife. "Yes, she is." He asked many questions about my relationship with my father-in-law, the children, my work and to each one Ernest could only answer, "She is the best."

Finally, the lawyer looked at him and said, "Why do you want a divorce?"

"Because she nags me."

He turned to me and asked the same questions, much in the same way, ending by asking, "Why do you want to leave him?"

I replied, "He is not ambitious enough for me."

With his eyes full of concern and caring, he smiled. He shook his head and said, "You two hold hands now and get home, grow up and never come back to me again." We left, our marriage back on track.

Ernest began to think more of our future. He knew

he had to return to the medical field of opthalmology in which he had been trained, but he was still obligated to finish his contract in Pueblo. After the war ended in September of 1945, it was time for Ernest to start looking. He heard of a job in Marshall town, Iowa at the Wolf Cataract Clinic. His contract was for one year only, until Dr. Wolf's son completed his tour of military duty. It stipulated that at the end of his year with the Wolf Clinic that he would not set up a practice within a 200-mile radius "as the crow flies." It seemed impossible to consider settling in Iowa for good so we began to look at Missouri, where he had been certified originally. We knew that we couldn't afford to live in Kansas City or St. Louis but we were very interested in Springfield. We didn't know anyone there, but that was nothing new for us.

We contacted Rabbi Ernest Jacob in Springfield and told him we were coming to find out about the possibilities of settling there. The rabbi told us that he didn't know much about the medical field in Springfield but invited us to be his guests for a few days. He too, was a former refugee. We liked the city, but didn't realize that all the doctors who had left to go to war would be returning soon, having been promised their office space when they came back. It seemed hopeless until we heard that Mr. Heer, a prominent business man, had one office open in the Woodruff Building that was available. I personally went to him and explained our previous years, the hardships we endured under Hitler and how hard we had worked to keep our family together. Mr Heer looked at me and said, "The office is yours."

The Second major difficulty was that we had no money to rent a house. Our little savings would go to furnish the office. We returned to Iowa and talked to our friends. They pooled their resources and offered to lend us several hundred dollars to get us started, on the condition that we would pay back the money as soon as we could. We came to Springfield and rented a house on the north side of town on Calhoun Street for forty-five dollars a month. Our family was small, Ernest, Papa, the children and I, and we barely had any furniture. The house was a two-story with two bedrooms upstairs and one downstairs for Papa. I did the best I could with the old furniture we had and I was sure that there had never been a more beautiful home---or one in which I felt more secure. Maybe it was this moment that I felt my fear began to loosen its grip on my life. It never occurred to me that no other doctor lived on the north side of town. We were able to buy the house for $3500, and to me, that made us millionaires. We were happy and our family prospered.

Ernest bought his office equipment on credit, opened the office and waited for patients. His first patients were two nuns from St. John's Hospital. Remembering the nuns who had risked imprisonment or worse to come to treat my mother in Germany, Ernest treated them for free. Two priests appeared the next day, insisting on paying. The money was meager. We were total strangers in town and we knew there had to be a way to get known by the population. Once more, Ernest's second profession of music came to our rescue. He started performing for various civic organizations such as the University Club, Rotary Club and the Optimists Club. Everybody loved his music and the demand for his performances was overwhelming. And people who heard him play began to find their way to his office, thinking anyone that gifted must also be a good healer. We began to make enough money to repay the loan from our good friends in Iowa. Life was good.

CHAPTER 11
Our Family Grows

A year after we moved to Springfield, David was born. He really wasn't planned, but having been an only child, I was delighted at our growing family. David was so special. He was sweet and considerate and one of his favorite things was giving out "colored kisses." He might give a red, blue, yellow or green one, each with a special loving meaning. As was common with older brothers, Tony was the only person who could make David mad. He was eight years older and stronger and smarter. David dreamed of the time when he would be sixty-two and Tony, seventy because he was planning on beating him up then!

When David was about four, I lost my beloved Papa, one of the dearest friends I thought I would ever know. Except for losing Papa, this time, when my children were young, was the best time of my life. I cooked, cleaned and shared wonderful times with them. The entire family played games together. Ernest took time to play the piano at least three hours a day and sometimes even longer. For years, the children fell asleep to daddy's beautiful music. I made new friends, had coffee with the neighbors, in general lived like people were meant to live, without oppression, hopelessness or despair---maybe without fear. I was beginning to learn to live without fear and I was never more content.

CHAPTER 12
Our Jewish Life

Through the years Ernest had made sure that we celebrated all Jewish holidays and that we kept Judaism as an important part of our lives. We had never lived anywhere with a large enough Jewish community to keep our religion with other Jews. We had tried to keep it in our home and our hearts. The years of the Holocaust were deeply embedded in our minds. He led the Passover Seder for many years. He had special gifts for the family on Hanukkah. We always lit the candles on Friday night and blessed them, drank the wine and blessed the bread for our Sabbath. We knew that we were Jews and were proud of it. We never envied Gentiles for their Christmas, we had our own holidays and celebrated in the tradition of our forefathers. And it was Ernest who gave us the amazing gift of music for our holidays. He gave us our love and appreciation of the richness of Judaism through his playing. He was the organist at Temple for years because he felt it was very important to share his talent with his people. He never missed playing on Friday nights, even when he was very ill with cancer. He even left his hospital bed to play for the services.

Although we did not follow all of the Jewish traditions, Ernest had a deep love for his religion and great feelings for Israel. One of his most emotional moments was when we visited the Wailing Wall in Israel. I could not share this with him because my father had died so early, when he was fifty-four, and my mother never practiced. It might have been different if my father had lived but fortunately I had Ernest who taught me the depths of Judaism and awakened my pride in my heritage.

We felt so lucky that we decided it was time for us to give back---to do something for someone who was less fortunate than ourselves. Herbert Palm was the son of Ernest's best friend in Dusseldorf. His Jewish father had been killed in a concentration camp but his mother was a gentile so they were able to make their way to America. We wrote to her and she told us that she was barely able to take care of herself and her fourteen year old son. We decided that Herbert should come and live with us for a year. He was a frightened, colorless boy who was entirely submissive. His mother must have told him to be a good boy while he was with us and he took it to heart. He was almost too sweet. He completed all the tasks that I gave to my children which, of course, they resented. They simply never got to like him. He went to Pipkin Junior High School where he took endless teasing from other boys until we gave him boxing lessons at the Boy's Club. He gained some degree of confidence and strength and when he left at the end of the year he seemed to have lost some of his submissiveness and stood up for himself a little more.

We read a newspaper article by Eleanor Roosevelt about the three most badly treated European Jewish youngsters she had ever seen. All three had suffered incredibly under the Nazis. She described the case of a Jewish girl in Vienna who, at the age of six was thrown down three flights of stairs in an apartment building and remained sickly for many years. I got together with Annie Jacob, our rabbi's wife, and we decided to send Care packages to this girl and her family. After we had kept that up for twelve years and also sent money for heat and utilities, I thought it was time to do something special for Edith. The cost of a flight from Vienna to Springfield was about three hundred dollars. At that time we had a newspaper called "BIAS." I put an article in the paper telling people about Edith, suggesting that if people would contribute one dollar each we could make it a wonderful year for this teenager. The money was collected in just a few days. We ended up with over four hundred dollars and now we could bring Edith over for a whole year, a year in which she could learn English and maybe a trade. This girl had never been out of her district, never been anywhere. She was an interpreter for her mother, who was very hard of hearing. Her father had been so badly beaten by the Nazis that he was an invalid. We found out the name of her doctor in Vienna, told him the story and he went to the family and pleaded with them to let Edith go. She was so excited that she packed her suitcase with very few clothes and started on her voyage to America.

Edith had so much courage and so much youthful spirit, but like me, she didn't venture out of her cabin for three days. Also like me, she found many new friends and bonded with them rapidly. She arrived in New York where my cousin Claire picked her up. She called us, letting us know that she was in no condition to take the bus all the way to Springfield, Missouri. We had to give her at least a week to recuperate. After one week, Edith arrived in Springfield on the bus and met her new American family. We were so nervous, not knowing who was coming to join us. We were stunned when a beautiful young girl got off the bus. We took her home and showed her our house. She was overcome. It was a palace to her. She took five showers a day, having never showered before. She was used to going to a communal bathhouse in Vienna. She ate everything in the icebox and I loved her from the first moment I saw her. She understood me better than my own children because of our similar experiences in Germany. She became the darling of Springfield. People all wanted to meet the girl their dollar had brought to America. She had no trouble getting into school, though her English was practically nil. She found a summer job at Rubenstein's selling clothes. Everybody liked her accent, charm and brightness.

My own children were not so crazy about her. They thought they had lost their mother. I pleaded guilty to their charges and for one year my feelings were put above those of David, Tony and Eleanor. I hope that by now they have forgiven me but I felt that I had to make up for the gruesome events Edith had lived through. With good and free medical care she blossomed. During the time Edith was with us in 1955, I turned forty-two and found out I was pregnant again. I was delighted! I went to the doctor's office with all the young mothers and felt as young as they. I wished for nothing else but to have a healthy baby. I hoped for a girl. My wish was granted and my darling Mimi was born January 14, 1956. I guess I dreaded the thought of another boy because I was never interested in sports---I had attended enough baseball games the summer before to last me a lifetime. After Mimi was born my concentration was not focused so totally on

Edith. Mimi's older siblings adored her and to her father she became the sunshine of his later years.

When the year was over for Edith, the doctor in Vienna wrote us that her parents were very ill and she needed to return. One of our concerns about bringing her to America had been sending her back to the misery of her prior existence but we fooled them all--- she went back healthy and strong, knowing what she wanted. She now had a good command of the English language and returned to Vienna with the courage to handle life on her own. Her first job was in a candy store frequented by lots of American soldiers. She talked to them about peanut butter, the Ozarks, America and she made so many friends that the store was filled with young soldiers. She met a musician from Canada who was on a scholarship in Vienna to study music and they fell in love. Two or three years later they married and had a beautiful apartment where they entertained the most prominent musicians from all over Europe. She became a star, this girl who came from nothing. When we visited her sometime later, we were treated like royalty.

THIRTEEN
I Go Back To School and
Find a New Profession

We had lived on Calhoun Street for many years when we realized that though we loved our house, the neighborhood was beginning to deteriorate and we needed to think about moving. All of our friends and Ernest's professional associates lived on the south side of town. We eventually bought a piece of property which was located in south Springfield on Langston Street. Very few houses had been built there at this time and a friend, Winslow Ames, the curator of the Art Museum drew up the plans for our house. I could hardly believe, as a former refugee who had been kicked from country to country, that I could actually own a piece of land with plans to build such a fine house. However, we had to be patient and wait until we were financially able to build.

While we were still on Calhoun Street, Ernest bought an old Chevy for me with 135,000 miles on it which I considered my Cadillac. I had taken a driver's test before in hopes that I would someday own a car. My car gave me mobility and I had time to think of myself, since all three of our children were in school and Mimi hadn't been born yet.

What I wanted to do was go to school and get a degree in early childhood education. I went to Southwest Missouri State University and took the entrance exam which showed I had an IQ of 60. Because I seemed so determined, the college decided to allow me to attend even with that very low score but put me on probation. After six months the dean called me to his office and told me he could not understand my low IQ since I was an excellent student and aced many of my classes. I told him that I had never taken such an exam before and didn't know that I was being timed so I only finished half the paper. He smiled and said that the probation was lifted.

I felt strange in school. I was already forty years old and everyone else was so young but I was able to hold my own. A year and a half went by and I found myself pregnant again. I finished up the school year and went back to being a house frau and a new mother again. I was determined to find a job and eventually I found my way to Springfield Demonstration Kindergarten and Preschool. I talked with the owner, Minnie Lee Lemons, and asked her if I could bring my guitar and play and sing for the children. I could also teach the recorder, an older flute-type instrument. Minnie was glad to have me as a volunteer and with each passing month she gave me more responsibilities. Mimi

63

was two and a half and I could bring her to school with me. I loved the children and they loved me. However there was no way Minnie could employ me on a paying basis since I had not finished my degree. When her associate, Mrs. Harmon became unable to work she called me to take her place.

After many years of working at the school, Minnie Lee Lemmons, a beautiful, creative person retired and a new administrator took her place. The new administrator was totally unimaginative. Everything that I had brought to the school that was creative, she hated. She never supported any of my ideas and one day I got so angry with her that I took my guitar and left. Then I started receiving letters from many of the parents who had enjoyed my teaching and I was asked to start a school of my own. This was a wonderful idea but I had no money to build a school. I had to depend on a church that was willing to give me room for my preschool. It didn't take long for the Southminister Presbyterian to contact me and offer a merger. They had been talking about a preschool in their church and were interested in meeting with me. The minister and I liked each other and I was able to start my own school. I sent a letter out to some of the parents that I knew through Springfield Demonstration and within two weeks I had eighteen registrations. Since I knew nothing about running the business end of the school, I took in a partner, Charlotte Levitch, who helped me with the school and was an excellent bookkeeper.

One of the more creative things we did was to acquire an old truck which we painted with vibrant colors and placed in the yard for the children to play on. They loved sitting in the driver's seat and "driving" all around. While their contemporaries in other daycare centers were swinging on jungle gyms and swing sets, my little charges were climbing all over their own wonderful fantastic truck. Only one problem developed with our truck. It seems the neighborhood teens were also finding pleasure in the parked vehicle after hours. We decided it had to go, so our magnificent truck had to be dismantled.

As one would expect, music was an important part of the Tarrasch household. It ran through every fiber of our beings. Ernie and I were so very proud of all our children. Eleanor played the violin very young and eventually played in the Springfield Symphony as did David on the cello. Tony played the clarinet and Mimi, the flute. There were many "firsts" brought home from state music contests in Columbia. But the happiest hours our family spent together were those long summer evenings gathered around Ernie and his Yamaha grand piano, with all the windows open, our beautiful

65

music floating out our windows, sharing our music with all the residents of Langston Street.

FOURTEEN
Our Chinese Children

One day in the mid-50's, Ernest and I read in the newspaper of the plight of starving orphans in Hong Kong. The institutions that housed these children were overcrowded and many of the children were malnourished. Chinese families from mainland China had fled to Hong Kong when the Communist Party and Chairman Mao came into power in 1949. Poor families kept their sons but abandoned their daughters. The little girls were put into orphanages or left on the front steps of churches. Many died of starvation, some were crammed fifty to a room and many never left their cribs alive.

We knew that we were able to financially care for one or two children. We went through Social Services in Springfield and decided to put in our application for one Chinese girl. They, in turn, sent our application to International Social Services. At that time I was 43 and Ernest was 46. Although we had four children of our own, we both felt we owed two starving children their lives since we had escaped the horrors of the Holocaust gas chambers and the nightmares that took the lives of so many Jews.

The Hong Kong government did not care about

our ages or the fact that we were Jewish. The orphan-age immediately sent us a picture and description of a very sad-looking little girl who was a year and a half. Her father had brought her to the orphanage and never came back for her. They told us she had tuberculosis. Ernest and I decided that this was the little girl we could help and we signed a waiver that we knew of her dis-ease and would consent to the adoption anyway. We knew that tuberculosis was treatable in the early stages here in the U.S. We still had to wait a year and a half for her visa. We had no idea exactly when she would arrive and had planned a trip to Michigan to attend a summer music camp when we received a call from In-ternational Services that our new daughter would be arriving the next day at five o'clock. Eleanor and I flew immediately to Chicago and waited until the airplane arrived. Out of the plane came a beautiful Chinese social worker with several children. She put a scream-ing child in our arms, wished us good luck and reboarded the plane.

We looked down at this pathetic child who could not understand us. She was broken out in hives with allergies to the food on the plane and her hair had been literally hacked off with a bowl over her head. She was dressed like a little old Chinese woman and was so frightened she was shaking all over. The first thing we did was take her to a restaurant for breakfast. She ate everything that was given to her but kept the last two bites of bread in her hand for fear there would be no more...something many survivors had done in the camps. Everyone turned to look at her. We took her to a department store, bought her a pretty dress, shoes and socks and put her in front of a mirror. She did something that resembled a curtsy and a slow smile spread over her little face. We went to a hotel and put her in her crib to rest. Apparently she had never been kissed or hugged and she responded to our touches by screaming. Before she fell asleep, she rocked herself from side to side, always hitting the boards of the bed. She must have been sleeping on the floor and now felt confined. The bathroom toilet was also a frightening experience---maybe she was afraid we would flush her too. The language barrier kept us from reassuring her but we did our best to make her comfortable.

The next day Ernest arrived with Mimi, Tony and David to look at our new family member. We journeyed to Michigan to the summer camp and the child traveled well in the car---she must have thought it was her new home. You had to stand in line for food at the camp and she was always first in line. Everybody helped her and she was learning to smile more often.

She became the darling of the camp and lived it up. We decided to call her "Joy."

When our vacation was over we drove back to Springfield and Joy adjusted very quickly---even the bathroom! When we told her this was her new home we knew she had no idea what we were talking about. The language barrier was difficult but shortly afterward she began to learn English. This process was accelerated when I took her to Springfield Demonstration with me. She adjusted well and played nicely with the other children who were fascinated by her.

One wonderful story about Joy was the day I took her to the soda fountain in Crank's Drug Store. A very obese man was sitting on one of the stools and his backside sort of hung over and down over the seat. Joy went up to him and pinched him in the rear. He whirled around, furious, but she just smiled and curtsied. She had just never seen anyone so fat!

Unfortunately Joy was very jealous of Mimi. She wanted me all to herself but that couldn't be so she pouted and let me know in no uncertain terms that she wanted Mimi to go away. I thought maybe Joy felt unhappy at being the only Oriental in the family and I began to look into finding another little girl. The agency granted us permission and we received a picture of a little one and a half year old girl who would become our daughter Ginger. She had been only a few months old when she was abandoned on the steps of a church, wrapped in a blanket and taken to an orphanage. This information was in her papers. I could hardly wait to tell Joy about her new little sister. She didn't seem too happy, probably afraid she would lose her position in the family as the youngest. We hoped all would go well. The agency could not tell us when she would arrive, as before. Ernest and I had plans to go to Europe for three weeks and were really looking forward to it. David was now in college and had invited his friend Carson to go with him to Colorado during our vacation. They were going to use my car for the trip.

Our trip was interesting and wonderful but a few days before we were scheduled to come home we received a call from Springfield at three o'clock one morning to tell us that David and Carson had been hit by a drunken driver and in the terrible accident, Carson was killed instantly, and David's feet were broken but he was alive. Our other children at home had seen to it that David was brought home by air ambulance. Eleanor and Tony assured us that everything that could be done for David was taken care of and we should stay the last few days anyway.

We were devastated by the news and those last days

were horrible. I was so glad David was alive but felt terrible guilt to be feeling relief when my dear friend Betty Crumley had lost her only son Carson. It took me months before I could face the Crumleys. What could I say to them? I said nothing, just put my arms around them. These wonderful people did not complain about their tragedy, just asked about David. I found the courage to tell them about foreign adoptions. A little girl would not remind them of their son and children were still starving in Hong Kong. They could save a child and bring laughter and sunshine back into their lives. They decided to think about it and several months later they called me and told me that they had just received a picture of their new daughter. They said they would never get over their grief but that I had been right---the child was like a ray of sunshine in their home, and the future looked bright again.

So, once again, I learned a lesson which I already knew---one can never replace a child, but one can give love to another and bring joy to life again.

David was depressed for a long time while his broken feet healed and he had to sit in a wheelchair. We all helped him but what helped him the most was his music. He listened to classical music hour after hour and he soon took on the role of conductor. He would lead the orchestra from their softest playing to the melodramatic heights, keeping himself busy for hours, conducting the great works as he healed.

Ginger arrived in Chicago but I couldn't pick her up because of David. A good friend, Betty Miller, met her plane in Chicago and brought her to our house. Betty was a fairy godmother to Ginger and she made life so exciting for her that Joy again became jealous. She eventually realized that I loved her enough to always try to make her happy and she began to feel more confident.

Since the Oriental children had no religion up to the time they came into our Jewish home, we followed our traditions and took them to Kansas City for a ritual bath, or mikvah, which was not available in Springfield. Immersion in the mikvah was part of their formal conversion to Judaism. I am sure they had no idea what was going on, but we celebrated and told them that they were now a part of our Jewish family. After all, they came over as refugees just as we did. Now our family was completed. I was forty-seven and Ernest was 50. The children kept us young and we had many happy---and sad---years with them.

FIFTEEN
Woman of the Year

One day in 1961, my friend Anne Drummond called
and invited me to lunch in the Crystal Room at the
Kentwood Arms Hotel. This was the most elegant ball-
room in Springfield at the time and I doubt anything
that has been built since surpasses it! You entered the
Kentwood with great respect and you dressed accord-
ingly. The entrance hall was elegantly furnished and
by using your imagination you could believe yourself
in a gorgeous European castle. Lunch matched the
decor in quality. We savored every bite and then sat
back and listened to Mayor David Scott who said we
were gathered to present three "Woman of the Year
Awards." A name with which I was very familiar, Dr.
Irene Coger, was called, and she went forward to get
her award for outstanding service in the field of the-
ater at SMSU. Productions of the drama department
were among the university's greatest accomplishments
and citizens of Springfield flocked to their performances. Many of these students went on to national
acclaim in the acting and directing fields.

Then, to my complete surprise, my name was
called! When I could get to my feet, my legs were shaking, my knees buckling and I heard the mayor say they

were presenting me the award for my "outstanding and unselfish devotion to the youth of Springfield."

I stood in shock beside Mayor Scott who, in kindness placed his hand on my shoulder and said loudly: "I know you could not have accomplished this alone: Jesus Christ was with you every step of the way."

I believe the mayor had simply forgotten I was Jewish, although I had given many talks in various churches where I spoke about the horrors of the Nazi regime.

As I returned to my seat, still week in the knees, I felt proud to hear the applause for someone who had been honored simply for bringing music and happiness into the lives of disadvantaged children. I was very much aware that the award had been precipitated by the McLaughlin Youth Center and the local Optimist Club. I also felt grateful to my delightful helper, Becky Hoover, a niece of the late Dr.Lee Hoover, who assisted me so faithfully for so many years.

This was another of those moments when I could feel all the fear and horror of my early years slipping away. My life was filled with all the happiness anyone could ask for. My mother would be pleased. Maybe she was at rest at last.

SIXTEEN
The Boat People

For many years life was smooth and interesting. The older children left home and, at the age of fifty-two, I was still enjoying my three remaining daughters. In 1978 and 1979, the newspapers were full of the plight of the Vietnamese Boat People, refugees who had fled from the communists in Vietnam by boat to camps in Indochina. While at sea, pirates robbed them of everything they had, sparing only their lives.

I knew only too well how difficult the life of a refugee can be. Had I not waited two years for a sponsor to bring me to America? It seemed to me that it was my time and obligation to help. What better way to repay all the people who had been good to me than to pass some assistance along to others in their time of need? I got in touch with the Council of Churches, and, with their help, was able to sign affidavits for twenty-three Vietnamese people within two years. We did not have much money but I asked many people to help me financially with this project and nobody ever turned me down. I received a great deal of help from my good friends Paul and Judy Mignard, whose help was invaluable.

My first family, Huoi, Bong and Chan came on February 18, 1980 on a cold and wintry day. They wore summer clothes and sandals, were without suitcases and spoke no English. The first thing I did was get in touch with the owners of Busy Bee clothing store. Mark Rosen outfitted everybody with warm clothing and appropriate shoes. All twenty-three refugees did wonderfully well within a short time in Springfield. The ones who attended SMSU were excellent students. The others worked in restaurants, cleaning establishments and anywhere else they could find work. Rarely were any of them on welfare and none of them disappointed me. They all justified my faith, confidence and trust and I felt my mission was accomplished.

Dedication

The last chapter of my memoirs I dedicate to the people other than my wonderful family who have done so much for me. I have appreciated their help and treasured their friendship. I like to think of them as my beautiful flowers, put in a magic vase which would preserve them for me through all of my life.

Dr. Robert Murney who helped me successfully overcome my many phobias once and for all.

The late Winslow Ames and all his family who helped me to think of people as being good instead of evil.

Dr. Gerrit tenZythoff who became my hero by having saved Jewish lives and who had been badly beaten in the concentration camps for hiding Jews in his cellar.

The whole Lotven family who were always there for me when I needed them---and I needed them often!

The late Rabbi Ernest Jacob and his wife Annette who understood my fears and anxieties, since they themselves were Nazi victims.

And my darling friend and coworker, Tina Nuccitelli, who was the star of my school and who gave so much love to the children.

In conclusion, I can now answer the question of why I survived the Holocaust; so many people have helped me, if in return, fate put me in the right time and place to help others in distress, then this is the reason my life was spared.

And why I can finally say farewell to fear--- today and always.

Epilogue
by Thel Spencer

Before relating what is currently going on in the life of Ena Tarrasch, a little background is in order. I met Ena in the fall of 1994 when we were involved in a daytime book-reading group attended by about half a dozen ladies from the Unitarian-Universalist Church and Ena Tarrasch. She mentioned to me, a writer of memoirs, that she had written her life story and wondered if I would take a look at it. I was just a few months away from publishing my second set of memoirs and was looking for another project, so I welcomed the assignment and dropped by her house a few days later to pursue the matter.

Nothing I had ever experienced in a lifetime of reading people's stories prepared me for the exhilaration I felt when I curled up on the sofa that evening and began to read what I later decided to title <u>Farewell to Fear</u>. Excitement began to build with the early statements about fear---when I tried to recall what my own earliest memories of fear were like---and it continued as Bettina Kaff faced each problem she encountered with courage and tenacity. It was not until she was safely on board the Aquatania and on her way to America that I was able to breathe a sigh of relief. I am very pleased to have had even a small part in the un-folding of Ena's marvelous story.

We worked together for months as 1994 turned into 1995. Shortly before the end of the year, I had occasion to be on the phone with Bob Glazier, editor of Springfield Magazine, about the stories I was working on and casually mentioned that I had the story of Ena Tarrasch. There was silence on his end of the line. Then, in a voice hushed with a sort of reverence, he said "You have the story of Ena Tarrasch?"

Holding my breath, I replied "Yes."

From Editor Glazier, "You mean the Ena Tarrasch, the wife of Ernest Tarrasch, Doctor Ernest Tarrasch?"

It was not until that moment that I fully comprehended what I had in <u>Farewell to Fear</u>. I replied in the affirmative and Editor Glazier lost no time in arranging an appointment for us to come to his office to talk about serializing Ena's memoirs in his magazine. Ena was elated at the prospect of being published, but totally unprepared for the delay of the year that followed before the first issue appeared in February of 1996. I was also pleased with a later issue in which Editor Glazier discussed her story in his column "Inside Spring-field:"

"Probably the most discussed series of articles ever to appear in this magazine is Thel Spencer's <u>Farewell</u>

to Fear, the autobiography of Springfieldian Ena Tarrasch, who makes it to the altar in this installment only to find her pursuit of happiness interrupted by phobias and nightmares from her earlier days in Nazi Germany."

Farewell to Fear is an important addition to the holocaust genre and will be first published in hardcover in the spring of 1997. As we near this date, it seems only fair to her readers that they be informed of Ena's current activities. She continues to house foreign students in her home---Japanese Naoki Miki being her current companion and an absolute joy (I have noticed that each student who occupies her spare room surpasses his predecessor in virtue).

Ena is an active member at the new Temple Israel, recently erected on property southeast of Springfield out Route 60 on Farm Road 193. Three mornings a week will find her at the water aerobics class she takes at the Hammons Heart Institute. She attributes her good health these days to the regular exercise she gets in this activity; notwithstanding the fact that she underwent open heart surgery with four bypasses a year ago.

Tuesday evenings will usually find Ena with her Recorder Group of the Ozarks when about seven musicians converge on her music room and play the look-like-flute instruments that range from one foot to three feet in length. They have been playing together for 35 years and the only other member of the original group who attended the first session with Ena is Dr. Richard Mears.

The three other members of the bridge group she attends once a week say she plays an excellent game of bridge despite the fact that she has been known to trump her partner's trick or chicken out of a finesse on very rare occasions. But haven't we all?

Volunteer work at the new blood center keeps taking up Ena's time. As a board member and volunteer at the Jewish Community Center she helps out by setting up tables and preparing food. After ten years she retired from being a volunteer visitor at the Medical Center for Federal Prisoners when her favorite inmate, a man named Sendoni, was shipped back to Italy only to be murdered---an event Sendoni had predicted. But Ena remembers only the positive things about the charming man: how he kissed her hand in European-style greeting, how she would buy him coffee at the canteen and spread a napkin and set the table with silverware, behaving as graciously as possible. She never heard the number of persons he had "taken out," but he was always a gentleman to her.

The Rosenbaum store on the north side of Park

Central Square in Springfield is a long-established part of the business community, having been in business since the '70's. Recently in the store to make a purchase, I asked the Rosenbaum brothers the rhetorical question of whether they knew Ernest Tarrasch. They admitted to not only being friends of Ernest's but also distant relatives. That is, they said their mothers were distant relatives. Once the subject had been broached, Larry Rosenbaum began relating, in non-stop stand-up-comedian-style, stories of their families' long association. Here, undoubtedly, was a man who knew and loved Ernest Tarrasch.

At that precise moment the idea of writing the life story of Ernest Tarrasch occurred to me. So that <u>Farewell to Fear</u>, going to press in the spring of 1997 will be followed by <u>Hello Happiness</u>, and readers will be lavishly entertained with recountings on the light side submitted by the family and friends of Ernest Tarrasch as told to Thel Spencer. The sequel is also to be published by Denlinger's Publishers, Ltd., of Centreville, Virginia.